ELECTRICITY IN ACTION

# THAT'S SHOCKING!
## ELECTRICITY IN NATURE

by Jenny Mason

CAPSTONE PRESS
a capstone imprint

Published by Capstone Press, an imprint of Capstone
1710 Roe Crest Drive, North Mankato, Minnesota 56003
capstonepub.com

Copyright © 2026 by Capstone. All rights reserved. No part of this publication
may be reproduced in whole or in part, or stored in a retrieval system, or
transmitted in any form or by any means, electronic, mechanical, photocopying,
recording, or otherwise, without written permission of the publisher.

Library of Congress Cataloging-in-Publication Data is available on the Library of
Congress website.

ISBN: 9798875222382 (hardcover)
ISBN: 9798875222337 (paperback)
ISBN: 9798875222344 (ebook PDF)

Summary: Electricity exists everywhere in the universe. Find out how Earth,
the sun, the sky, plants, animals, and even your body make and use electricity.

Editorial Credits
Editor: Ashley Kuehl; Designer: Sarah Bennett; Media Researcher: Rebekah
Hubstenberger; Production Specialist: Tori Abraham

Image Credits
Alamy: Science History Images, 26; Getty Images: BSIP/Universal Images
Group, 28, Ed Reschke, 21, Ger Bosma, 18, iStock/Al Carrera, 13, iStock/artorn,
14, iStock/HansJoachim, 8, iStock/keiichihiki, 17, iStock/Sander Meertins, 7,
iStock/Vitalii Dumma, 25, MARK GARLICK/SCIENCE PHOTO LIBRARY,
11, RBFried, 23, Stephen Frink, 12, Westend61, cover, Yiming Chen, 19;
Shutterstock: Abstract51, 4, Alekseykolotvin, 9 (pie tin), BlueRingMedia, 10,
Dennis van de Water, 20, John Carnemolla, 16, Lavrentev Vladimir, 9 (fork),
MattL_Images, 29, New Africa, 27 (dominoes), SNAPSY, 15, Veniamin Kraskov,
9 (sock), Yuphayao Pooh's, 27 (string)

Design Elements
Shutterstock: galihprihatama, Iurii Motov

Any additional websites and resources referenced in this book are not
maintained, authorized, or sponsored by Capstone. All product and company
names are trademarks™ or registered® trademarks of their respective holders.

Printed and bound in China.  006276

# Table of Contents

**INTRODUCTION**
NIGHT FLASHES . . . . . . . . . . . . . . . . . . . .4

**CHAPTER 1**
FLASH, FLICKER, GLOW . . . . . . . . . . . . . . .6

**CHAPTER 2**
TINGLERS, ZAPPERS, BUZZERS, AND MORE . . . . . .12

**CHAPTER 3**
BOLTS THROUGH YOUR BODY . . . . . . . . . . . .22

GLOSSARY . . . . . . . . . . . . . . . . . . . .30
READ MORE . . . . . . . . . . . . . . . . . . .31
INTERNET SITES . . . . . . . . . . . . . . . . .31
INDEX . . . . . . . . . . . . . . . . . . . . 32
ABOUT THE AUTHOR . . . . . . . . . . . . 32

Words in **bold** are in the glossary.

## INTRODUCTION
# NIGHT FLASHES

In 2024, neon green and pink ribbons danced across night skies. You might know these glowing auroras as the Northern Lights. Normally, they appear near Earth's poles. But in 2024 they stretched almost to the equator!

Auroras reveal the electricity that exists everywhere in the universe. It is inside stars, planets, plants, insects, animals, and even you! Discover how the energy that powers your video games is the same juice that pumps your heart!

# WHAT'S THE BUZZ ON ELECTRICITY?

## What is electricity?

Electricity is a natural force. It can be used to make light and heat or to make machines work.

## Where does electricity come from?

Everything in the universe is made of super-tiny building blocks called **atoms**. Each atom has **protons**, **neutrons**, and **electrons**. Sometimes, electrons can move from one atom to the next. That movement creates electricity.

## What's the difference between a conductor and an insulator?

Electricity moves through **conductors**. Conductors are materials that help electrons flow easily. Water and certain metals are conductors. **Insulators** slow or stop the flow of electrons. Wood, plastic, and rubber are insulators.

## How is electricity measured?

Amps tell you how quickly the electrons are moving. Volts tell you how much pressure there is on the electrons. The energy of electricity can be put to work. The difficulty of the work is measured in watts.

### Watts = Amps x Volts

## CHAPTER 1

# FLASH, FLICKER, GLOW

Lightning is probably nature's best-known electric display. But how do storms create electricity?

First, water, dust, and air particles swirl and collide to create **friction**. Normally, magnetism holds protons and electrons together. But this friction pulls them apart, building up an electric charge. Because electrons have the same negative charge, they repel each other.

Air is an insulator. For a while, it traps the electrons. When the charge grows too big for the air to hold, electrons burst out and leap to the nearest protons. The ground is naturally full of protons. The electrons form a bolt of lightning that usually connects to the ground.

### FACT

Lightning can also form inside a cloud without escaping to the ground. Or it can pass between clouds as charged protons in one cloud attract charged electrons in another.

# The Lightning Stone

Ancient people believed amber was magical. Amber is formed from fossilized tree sap. Rub it on fibers and it sparks. Or it can magnetically attract small objects. Electricity is named after an old word for amber: *elektron*.

# Create a Lightning Storm

Make your own thunderstorm at home! You'll need an adult's help for this activity.

## Supplies:

- a tack
- a disposable pie tin
- a pencil with an eraser
- a wool sock or cloth
- a Styrofoam plate
- a metal fork
- a light bulb

## Steps:

1. Poke the tack up through the center of the pie tin. Press the pencil eraser onto the tack's point. Make sure the pencil stands straight up.

2. Rub the wool over the plate for several minutes to build up a charge. Set the pie tin on the plate. Use the pencil as a handle.

3. Turn off the lights. Slowly bring the fork to the edge of the pie tin. Listen for a zap and watch for the bolt! Next, try using the light bulb instead of the fork.

4. What happens when you rub the plate longer?

## Earth's Electric Bubble

    Electricity is also generated deep inside Earth! Earth has a hard outer crust. Inside that is liquid metal. As the gooey metals slosh and churn, they generate electricity. Electric energy produces magnetic energy. The magnetic forces whoosh out of Earth's south pole. They wrap around the globe and dive back in near the north pole. This forms a protective bubble, or magnetic field, around Earth.

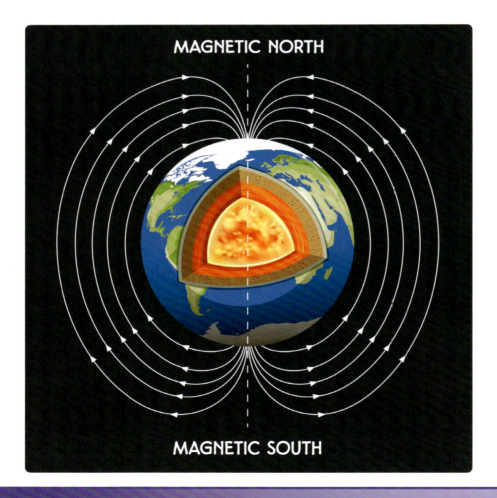

The sun constantly blasts outer space with hot gusts, like a hair dryer. The magnetic field keeps Earth's air in place. Huge explosions in the sun shoot charged particles through the solar system. Most bounce off the magnetic field. This ignites gases in the atmosphere and causes auroras.

In 1859, a solar storm pierced the magnetic field. Electric systems went haywire. In 1989, a strong flare damaged space satellites and fried power grids in Canada.

### FACT

Humans do not detect the magnetic field. But whales, migrating birds, bees, and mole rats use the magnetic energy to find their way.

## CHAPTER 2
# TINGLERS, ZAPPERS, BUZZERS, AND MORE

How do fish find their way in dark water? Many reach out with tingling electric pulses. About 350 fish species generate electricity to feel their environment.

Sharks, rays, and small skates use special pores to sense electric energy in the water. The pores might be on their snouts or heads.

In some fish, special organs near the tail generate about one volt. That's less than a AA battery. The organ holds hundreds or thousands of electrocytes. These cells mix chemicals to create electric energy. That energy pulses into the water around the fish. It creates an energy bubble. The fish finds food and friends through zing-detecting cells in its skin.

The stargazer fish has an organ behind its eyes that makes electric shocks.

## Zappers

Electric eels use electricity to communicate and find their way. They also use it to hunt! Once they detect prey, they blast out powerful shocks. The shocked prey twitches. These movements expose its hiding spot. The shock can even stop prey from swimming away. The eel connects its head and tail to the prey completing an electric circuit. It electrocutes the prey and eats it whole!

Electric catfish can produce up to 350 zapping volts.

### FACT

The electric eel generates up to 800 volts of electric charge!

## One Eely Good Idea

Alessandro Volta modeled his voltaic piles on eel electrocytes. In 1800, he stacked discs of metal and moist paper to make the world's first batteries. Modern inventors have created gooey batteries that stretch and bend just like real electrocytes.

## Pulse Hunters on Land

Most tinglers live in water. But two live at least partly on land. One is the platypus. It hunts in water. Its duck-like bill has 40,000 electroreceptors. These cells sense electric signals made when prey moves or breathes.

A swimming platypus catches a worm.

Echidnas eat mostly ants and termites.

The echidna, the platypus's cousin, lives on land full time. This mammal has between 400 and 2,000 electroreceptors in its snout. The snout "sees" through the ground and digs up a juicy dinner! Echidnas and platypuses are the only mammals that lay eggs. These unique animals also have pouches like kangaroos.

## Best Foot Forward

Geckos use electric forces to walk at any angle, even upside down! A gecko's toes have thin, hair-like stalks called setae. The setae spread across any surface. They are so small, they push electrons away from protons. Scattering these particles creates an attraction force that seals the gecko's feet to the surface!

The strips of tissue on a gecko's foot, called lamellae, are made of many clusters of setae.

# Be a Gecko!

Want to imitate a gecko's powers? Try this experiment!

**Supplies:**
- 2 Styrofoam plates
- a wool cloth or sock
- a table

## Steps:

1. Rub the wool over one plate for a couple of minutes. Set the plate facedown on a table.

2. Hold the second plate by its edge and try to set it on the first plate. Observe what happens.

3. Hold one hand, palm down, 3 to 4 inches (7.5 to 10 centimeters) above the first plate. Insert the second plate into the gap and let it drop.

4. Bounce your hand up and down. What happens?

About 60 percent of the world's 1,500 gecko species can stick to surfaces. That includes the gold dust day gecko.

## Tiny Electrical Wonders

Bees use electricity to gather food from flowers. As they fly, their bodies gather extra protons from the air. They develop a positive charge. Soil is negatively charged. That causes plants in the soil to build up a negative charge. When a bee lands on a flower, pollen leaps onto the bee's fuzz. Bees can detect when flowers have no pollen because they those flowers have no charge!

The yellow cells on oriental hornets are actually solar panels! They convert sunlight into energy for the hornet.

Electrons in pollen are attracted to the protons on a bumblebee.

### FACT

Spiders use electricity too. They weave electric webs. The web strands are negatively charged. When an insect gets close, the web strands jump toward it. They are attracted to the bug's positive charge!

# CHAPTER 3
# BOLTS THROUGH YOUR BODY

More than 200 years ago, Mary Shelley wrote *Frankenstein.* In the story, lightning jolts life into a monster made of human body parts. In 1818, the idea that human bodies ran on electricity seemed like fiction. Today, we know it's a fact! Your teeth, skin, blood, and organs are all part of your body's electrome, or electric systems.

Your body's cells act like tiny batteries. The cell's **membrane** separates ions, or charged atoms. A negative charge builds inside the membrane. Ions outside the membrane have a positive charge. The attraction between these opposites builds pressure. When a part of the body needs to take action, the membrane opens. Opposites collide! This electric energy powers your body and brain.

**FACT**

Your skin produces enough charge to power a light bulb!

## Beats and Slings

Your heart is a pump that never stops. Electrical pulses squeeze and release the heart's muscle bundles. Charged ions drive the heart's electricity. The energy passes from cell to cell. The heart's rhythm must be spot on. It makes the right amount of fuel flow through the body.

The brain's **neurons** sling electric bursts at high speeds. Neurons process information from your body's senses. They run your organs. Their electricity creates your thoughts and feelings!

### FACT
Each heart cell produces less than a volt of electricity. But the heart is made of several billion cells. Together they produce a lot of power!

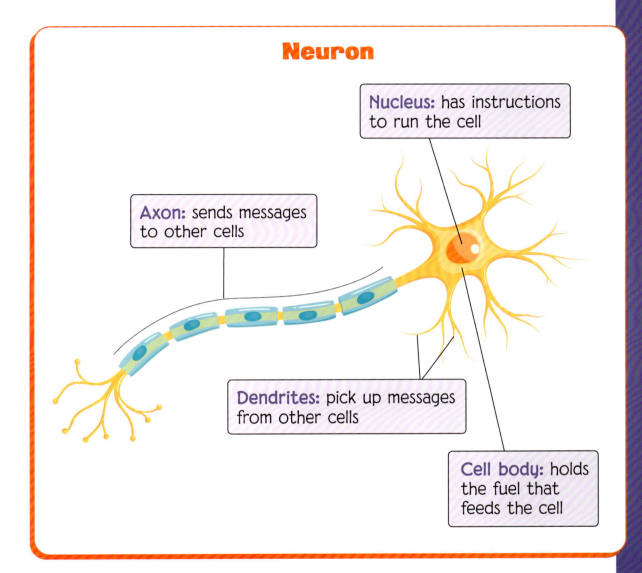

# Mind Blown

Santiago Ramon y Cajal loved drawing. He was a doctor in the late 1800s. He drew detailed images of cells. Ramon y Cajal's art led to the discovery that neurons moved electricity.

# Test Your Nerve

Neurons push electric signals through the brain and body. Use this experiment to see how fast they can go!

### Supplies:
- 5 rulers
- a set of dominoes
- a tape measure
- some string

### Steps:

1. Stand a domino upright under each end of every ruler. Arrange the rulers into one long straight line. Leave a gap the width of your finger between them. Imagine the rulers are neurons.

2. Arrange more dominoes in a line beside the rulers. Space the dominoes about an inch apart. Imagine these are your body's cells.

3. Use the tape measure to make sure the lines are equal in length.

4. Place the string at one end for a finish line.

5. Which moves electric signals faster: neurons or body cells? Tip the starting dominoes and watch the race!

6. Which cell was faster? Why might electric signals between your brain and body need to act fast?

Electricity crackles, flashes, and zaps everywhere. While we cannot always sense it, many animals and plants can. The electric powers of other animals help us invent better technology. Scientists continue finding ways to use electrical energy in medical treatments. Mastering the wildly wired world is critical to the survival of all Earth's species.

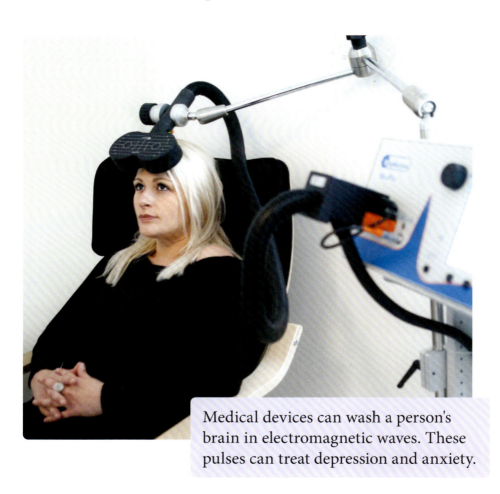

Medical devices can wash a person's brain in electromagnetic waves. These pulses can treat depression and anxiety.

# GLOSSARY

**atom** (AT-uhm)—an element in its smallest form

**conductor** (kuhn-DUHK-tuhr)—a material that lets electricity travel easily through it

**electrocute** (i-LEK-truh-kyoot)—to hurt or kill by electric shock

**electron** (i-LEK-tron)—a negatively charged particle that whirls around the nucleus of an atom

**friction** (FRIK-shuhn)—a force that is produced when an object rubs against another

**insulator** (IN-suh-late-or)—a material that blocks an electrical current

**membrane** (MEM-brane)—the thin outer layer of a cell

**neuron** (NOOR-ahn)—a cell that moves electric signals between the brain and other body parts

**neutron** (NOO-trahn)—a particle in the nucleus of an atom that has no electric charge

**proton** (PRO-tahn)—a positively charged particle in the nucleus of an atom

# READ MORE

Mallory, Louis. *Electric Eels Make Electricity!* Buffalo, New York: Gareth Stevens Publishing, 2024.

O'Daly, Anne. *Amazing Activities with Electricity and Magnetism.* New York: Enslow Publishing, 2022.

Temple, Colton. *Amazing Animal Electricity.* Minneapolis: Kaleidoscope, 2021.

# INTERNET SITES

*Hydro-Québec: Electricity in Nature*
hydroquebec.com/learning/notions-de-base/nature.html

*Operation Jimmy: Electricity in Nature*
operationjimmy.uk/find-out/electricity/in-nature.html

*Science Trek: D4K Electricity*
pbs.org/video/science-trek-electricity-2013/

# INDEX

amber, 8
atoms, 5, 22
auroras, 4, 11

batteries, 13, 15, 22
bees, 11, 20, 21

echidnas, 17
eels, 14, 15
electrome, 22
electrons, 5, 6, 7, 18, 21

fish, 12, 13, 14
friction, 6

geckos, 18, 19

hearts, 4, 24

lightning, 6, 7, 8, 9, 22

magnetic fields, 10, 11

neurons, 24, 25, 26, 27
neutrons, 5
Northern Lights, 4

platypuses, 16, 17
protons, 5, 6, 7, 18, 20, 21

Ramon y Cajal, Santiago, 26

spiders, 21

Volta, Alessandro, 15

# ABOUT THE AUTHOR

Jenny Mason is a story-hunter. She explores foreign countries, canyon mazes, and burial crypts to gather the facts that make the best true tales. She'll interview NASA engineers or sniff a 200-year-old skull. Her research knows no bounds! Jenny received her MFA in Writing for Children and Young Adults from the Vermont College of Fine Arts. She also holds a Master of Philosophy from Trinity College Dublin. Find all of Jenny's books and projects at jynnemason.com.